MIDNIGHT IN THE
CITY OF CLOCKS

Midnight in the City of Clocks

Tobias Hill

To Anne,
By the lake
Tyrone Guthrie Centre,
Summer 2005,

With best of luck & wishes,

Tobias Hill . x

OxfordPoets

CARCANET

First published in Great Britain in 1996 by Oxford University Press

This impression first published in 2004 by
Carcanet Press Limited
Alliance House
Cross Street
Manchester M2 7AQ

A CIP catalogue record for this book is available from
the British Library
ISBN 1 903039 76 2

The publisher acknowledges financial assistance from
Arts Council England

Printed and bound in England by SRP Ltd, Exeter

For George, Caroline and Amelia, my family

'Don't spend too much time with nightingales and peacocks.
One is just a voice, the other only colour'—Rumi

Acknowledgements

Acknowledgements are due to the editors of the following publications in which some of the poems in this collection first appeared: *Ambit, Apostrophe, The Bound Spiral, Connections, Envoi, The Frogmore Papers, The Independent, London Magazine, Northwords, The Observer, Orbis, Outposts, Pause, Poetry London Newsletter, London Quarterly, Poetry Review, Poetry Wales, Printed Matter, Quartos, Stand Magazine, Staple, Superreal, Tabla*.

Poems have been read on Radio 3 on National Poetry Day 1995 and in 'Best Words'. Previous pamphlets and limited collections include *Sestet* (Staple First Editions 1995), and *Year of the Dog* (National Poetry Foundation 1995).

Some of the poems formed part of a collection that received a major Eric Gregory Award in 1995. One was shortlisted for the Forward Prize 1995 (Best Poem). Individual poems also won, among other competitions, the 1995 Frogmore Prize and the 1995 Vers Poets Prize.

Contents

I

TRANSIT

The City of Clocks

Slaughter-month. The road is down
and the telephone clacks like knitting.
Departure is set back for days.
To kill the time, we memorise
phrasebook lines, or play mah-jong.
The pieces are made of bamboo
and sealbone, green as oxygen.
We monitor the radio
for facts. The static rises, falls.
I dream of pistons and sirens.

We are returning to the city
where every room has an echo,
each echo, pitch. Whistle right,
and walls thrum like wineglass,
crack. This is where I was born.
I pack a budget travel-guide,
keys and coins, plastic money.

All our maps are obsolete.
Along the oceanside, sinkholes
have cratered the old shopping-malls
with sea-caves, where waves slap like bombs
in the salt dark. The stone arcades
reek of sewage and bladderwrack.

The metro surfaces for this,
follows the racetrack and the ring-road
to an unattended station, lit
with blue Insectocutor light;
moths crack, burned to the metal grid.

This is our destination,
the city of clocks. Block your ears
and you can hear the watches tick
in syncopation with your heart.
No two clocks are ever in time.
If we hold hands, our pulses chat

against one another, like teeth,
gauging the distances we are apart.

Transit

She'd like to sleep. Letters of ice
scrawl a brittle alphabet
on the porthole-glass. Not English, but
a hard, white tongue
like English. She'd like to stop the sky's white noise.
She asks for one more tablet.

The wing is grey and shudders, sharp
as a scissor-blade or its absence
over the sequins of Bangkok's
fast cash and canals and light;
she wants to shred them, cut them out.

In-flight film. In Smoking, lights down,
the man with barcode hair
secretes his hand into her crotch,
snail's pace. Twists it tight.
She's junked-out, her face

crying as she dreams. He sees it;
her mistake. She'll pay for that.
Her tears are beautiful and shaped
like something poisonous; the sacs
of house-scorpions, the wasp's
syringe, the forcep-mouths
of white ants. She dreams

of running, trees. Pines, cage
on cage like helices. Only the earth
unbarred. Like an escape-route.

Prisons in a Departure Lounge at Midnight

The man with *Agent of Tai Wing Wa*
Hong Kong Lotus Seed Moon Cakes
printed on his coat is sleeping
on the bench by Duty Free. The cashier
looks the other way, expression
smeared across her cheeks.

He's curved and bunched like an intestine
over arm-rests, covering
shopping bags of caviar.
Around him on the airport floor
tiger-bone salesmen
play for vodka shots. Heads down,
they slap tricks on linoleum
and watch the youngest husband's woman
lie back
carved out
eyes shut

Upstairs in the Mile High Bar,
the night-shift air hostess drinks gin with ice,
redraws eye-shadows. Waits for flight.
She never licks her lips.
Lights go down in the arcades
where passengers for Ethiopia
sleep flat on newspapers, their plane
delayed for eighty hours.
The washroom shines with clothes hung out
to dry on walls and toilet doors.
An old man reads the Koran, pages
turned to catch the runway lights,
white beard left on like shaving foam.

The smell of acetone exhaustion
stains the plastic café seats
where thirty children sulk and cough
and cabin crews hand out ice-water,
jigsaws of Red Square at Noon,
posters to be coloured in,
500,000 Air Miles To be Won

Only the Duty Free is lit all night.
The cashier with blue cheekbones
behind the cage-block shutters, watching
seven televisions, listening
to Metal, headphones on.

I sit near to the moon cake man
where I can hear the smallbone crack
of screwtop bottles in her hands, and when
she half-sings, out of tune—

She turns, turns, trying selves.
Curls the furs against her thighs.
Outside, the hulks of aeroplanes
begin to move. She watches them
through high windows. Not stopping,
walking round and around the steel shelves.

7

One Day in Hiroshima

Hiroshima Noon

Peace Park. In the postwar trees
cicadas warm up like chainsaws.
The schoolchildren are out to catch them,
insect-cages on their arms
like handbags. Red plastic, green plastic.
Crowding up to reach the noise.

Nothing is happening today.
Watches are reaching noon
on the wrists of lunchbreak men.

There is a sound of aeroplanes
and the small creak of lawn-sprinklers.
Woods the horsemeat salesman
dozes on an iron bench, nylon legs splayed apart.

His slip-on shoes are getting wet.
Sun ticks off the grass as steam,
smoke, the smell of minerals.
He dreams of spring. Teeming rain.
Across the road in the petrol station

borders of hydrangea
bruise against the air, their fists
delicate as litmus paper.
Testing subsoil and heat
for acid and its violence.

Hiroshima Midnight

River town. Ghettos of mud
run out to the sea-roads
between the park of cenotaphs,
the statue to dead high-school girls,
the street of love-hotels. Night brings out
their addiction to the light.

Knuckles raw as pickled plums,
Mister Fatboy pours us out
cold rice wine. We have the same job.
We make money. That's our job.
The barclock in the Gourmet Globe
has stopped. I'm dying for a drink
again. I watch the late-shift cook

skin spring chicken like a glove.
Tomorrow is Day of the Dead, when
all her ancestors ride home
on the curved backs of eggplants.
She hears them now, their insistence
rattling the storm windows.
She washes up, watching the street
for fast cars. Gullwings, tailfins.
Brakelights shimmy along the tram tracks,
asphalt radiating heat
and the lost dog-feet of litter
skittering up Peace Street.

Down by the docks, where the jetsam is,
the summer fireworks begin before we can get through the
    crowd.
The dark is fused with a smell like zinc;
beer cans and fried octopus. Office men with redmeat faces
splay under the gingko trees,
waiting for the festival.
All along the waterfront, lights in water like barcodes.
The child running through the crowd in summer gown and Adidas

is overhung with fireworks.
She cranes, head back, to watch their fall,
their drift. Spectacles of smoke
flashlit, huge in the mid-dark.

Closing-time. Through my shoes
the road is still warm, and the air
against my eyes and teeth is dry
with gunpowder and river-dust.
Up near the Peace Dome's fairground skeleton,
someone is shouting at someone,

I can't understand what. Mister Fatboy
starts to cry. I help him home,
streets emptied out
with the smell of ozone
and the sepia of streetlights in each dark room.

from A YEAR IN JAPAN

May

Spring in the rush-hour train:
the ticket-man, sumo-fat
and hurrying. The frills of his uniform
confettied with blossom.
Cherry in the hat-band, plum-dark
in the splendid epaulettes.

Sunlight blinks between the hulks
of love-hotels. A pyramid, a Palace
of Versailles. Balconies
on the Garden Babylon
backlit, ivy polythene green.

The businessman in the next seat
reads graphic erotica. In each strip
vamps and rapes, demons. Thick
as a Shakespeare. He doesn't look
at the girl in the seat opposite,

though I watch her, safely sleeping.
Head back, and the sun filming
her face. How the eyebrows are raised
when she dreams. And beyond her, small
in a landscape of water,

the flash of a kingfisher
taking a clean kill
like a lit crack in carnival glass.

August

Between the rag-slap of docks
and the winch-creak of abbatoirs
she stops teaching me names for the flex
of her hand, for birds. In pairs,
alone, the warehouse men
go home. Quiet, faces down.

Later, the saké warm as milk,
she finds the word for them. 'Untouchables.'
'How could you tell?' She rubs her hands
against her jeans. 'Their clothes, the place.
Differences.' Their name means
Waste-people. They work
with blood, the filth of animals.

Summer: season of poisonings.
In the space of hours, kept meat
rainbows like blacktop puddle-scum.
Eggs are sucked light with hidden rot,
crack open to a curd of gold.
The fishmonger drinks turtles' blood,
it washes the heart clean and strong;
he recommends it, as he guts.

Evening. Next door a snakeskin hangs
nailed over the windowframe. Drifts
in the wind. Poison for ghosts
and sickness. Mosquitoes whine
and fall quiet with intention.

Down by the docks and abbatoirs
the workers sit by the sea-shrine,
dreaming of summer in Japan.

Sweating with slight fever, heads bent,
waiting for the night-shift siren.

October

She meets the train
at Burning Stone station,
red leaves in her pocket
and the river from the mountain
green as an eye.

The sun keeps rhythm
through the pines. The train beats time. She tells me that
her names translate as Three Eight Sweet One,
Sickle-Hand, and that her town
is famous for carrots, and that

the moon has no face in Japan,
but the shadow of a hare, leapt
from the arms of a god.

Later, under the sod-black trees
she hides her face against the wind
and asks me to teach her to kiss.

Homesickness

Beyond the rocks of Ephesus
the goatherd led us to a rise
of land over the distant sea.

There were a pair of tesserae,
one gold, one of a fine-grained blue,
disordered in the wind and dust.

There was no crisis there,
there was no heart. The eye searched
for patterns, and found only

a lame goat, sheltering
under the steep branches
of a eucalyptus,

Heelbone of the past.

Blood-red seaweeds drip
along that coast—

Not mine. Who wrote this line?
This is not mine to write—

Here. I am here. I am.
The moon is shining
and the frogs are singing.

Playing Japanese Chess with
the Elder Mrs Uchida

Between the ebb of dusk
and turn of night, mosquitoes
gentle as thistledown
alight from the violet air
and settle on my hands and in her hair.
She brushes them away, and mutters
at the choice of pawn or knight.

The wind across the dry field
carries the chinks of bats
like jewels. The coolness
forces us inside. The board
set on tatami mats. She opens windows,
loosens nets. Outside
the rice-farmers burn scrub
to stubble. Mars and Sirius
are dulled, and the moon
ages with dust. She sits.

'My husband is dead.'
'I'm sorry.
How old was he?'

Over the board, her eyes
predict, calculate. Her hands
are veined and livered,
tapping at a pawn
and moving on.
'He is dead.'

'We were married in Autumn.
We say "Autumn, when
the sky is high
and the horses getting fat".'
'What did he do?'
'He bought me red cicadas.
Closed in his hands, like this.

Like little birds. They sang
Me-me-.' Her smile works
against the drawn lines
of her features.

Taps, taps. Lancer. King.
'Now he is dead. The cicadas
will not sing again. Ever
ever.' The sky
accumulates darkness.

Sumo Wrestler in Sushi Bar

One salmon-egg, a boil or pearl,
sticks to his doll-lips. He presses it
flat with his elephant fingertips.

Licks it. The barclock is too thin
between minutes, and the floor-mat
learns flatness under his weight.
His thighs flop down like sunstruck apes.

The bulbed light of light-bulbs
illuminates a world born small
and weak, measured in niggling strips
of sour rice and naked turbot.

It leaves him speechless. When he gapes
he redefines the planet with
the head-width of a halibut,

inch-cuts of raw sardine
converted into shoals of sweat.
He orders in his little voice, then waits
for the submarine girth of a bluefin.

Earthquake, Osaka 1995

She leans the door against a wall.
Takes off her shoes. On the freezer is a bottle
of *Plum Orchard Fine Rice Wine*. In the freezer
is the smell of rice fused to clinker in a pot.
Next to the freezer is a hole.
Through it she can see the street:

a boy in shorts is selling cans of Coke.
A boy in jeans is drinking head-down to a puddle.
Between sirens, an old woman
is catching locusts with her hands
in an allotment of tea-green rice.

She wants to help them but the television
has been broken and her arm
hurts to the bone. She pours rice wine
into her mouth, up to the hard brim of her teeth.

It tastes of sour milk.
She fills a cup until meniscus
shivers like clockwork at the brink.

Green Tea Cooling

Noon. In the public park
there is a white scorpion
in the black knuckles
of a cherry-tree.
It waits without motion
in a frail cloud of blossom.
The sun trembles
over the yellow grass.

The gardener, buckle-backed
from decades in the rice-fields
takes the white scorpion
by its poised tail
smoothly, and kills it
on the side of a rock
with the flat of her hand.

'I want to go North.
To Hokkaido. To see the Ainu.'

'Ah, the Ainu. Our natives.
You do not see them
around here in this time.
They are all gone.'

'But in Hokkaido?'

'Perhaps some, in the North.
But here they are all gone.
Like ghosts. Really,
like snow.'

The green tea cools
in our two bowls, as hours pass
in the quiet shade
of the shopfront. Outside
the traffic lessens. Noon

is almost come. The heat
reaches towards
an equilibrium. A white scorpion
waits without motion
in a frail cloud of blossom.

The Barber's Daughter

With one clean movement
she slides the cutthroat open

with ease, as she would gut
a gulping fish. The foam
she smooths across my cheeks
is wet as sweat.

Her legs are warm
against my arm. 'You shouldn't shave.
You cut yourself. You should come here
always.' The knife
etches my jawline.
In the mirror

the old garage attendant
tipped back in the next chair
watches the small TV
where samurai fight
in a field of snow. Her hand is soft
as the razor. By the door

her grandfather sits in the glare
of neon and sunlight, reading
a comic book. His cheeks hollow
behind the gold dog-teeth.
When she leans close, her hair
covers my heart-beat.
'Grandfather was eaten
by the tiger-sharks
during the war.'

I close my eyes. Her breath
is blossom. Fingers trace
across my neck
and back. The TV
whines and shouts. Beside the door
he turns a page. Red neon
spreads in ripples
over the silence of his face.

Waiting

Before morning I'm waiting here,
drinking green tea by the red door.
In my pocket there are keys,
two pens, one emptied. One of the keys
opens a box in England. In the box
is my grandfather's microscope,

with iris-valves that wink and dilate
like snake-eyes, and chipped glass slides
of a sexless baby's head
small as my watch face; a foetus—

This is irrelevant. This is
relevant. The night-sky

goes down behind Wu's Viking Grill
and Beer Hall. Clouds move
like mountains. I wait.
Across Seven Stone Children Street,
the fishmonger's son carries tuna
by the cheeks, hooks up crabs.
He looks them over with the care
of a potter. Sour ash

lifts from the icing factory.
I scribble margin-notes. A bloody rash
of water spreads from the butcher's door.
The match-scratch of the first cicada
ignites the sun. By twelve o'clock

it's a cymbal-crash
in the high branches. My knuckles crack, hands
on the page, waiting to cut
the ventricles and heat of noon
with the tremor of a pen.

The Secret of Burning Diamonds

Bought from the marts of Amsterdam,
the city built on herring-bones,
where emeralds dug in Serendip
shone and stank of mullet-skin—

This one was the first to burn.
A diamond dull as the flat gel
of a cod's eye. Quoted as point eight
carats, colouring poor, brilliance
sub-poor. Smelling of mine-mud.
Heart-flawed, the merchants at Rialto said,
and wouldn't pawn it for a pipe.

Not for the rose-cut, this one,
its chandelier hatchmarked with cracks.
Curio, knick-knack, souvenir
from Orange. Forgotten in a pocket,
the strongest substance in the world:

diamond. A lock gaping for keys.
Open as glass, giving away
nothing. Not that the cut skin
is lacquered with hydrogen,
or that this clenched strength
will burn—

Lavoisier, the alchemist,
buys it in the Jewish Quarter
for the price of a sausage.
Later, he'll invent oxygen.

Rio in Carnival

The earth is hot,
the smell of blacktop
steaming in the rain is sweet
as meat and red lipstick. Coffee
and guarana churn up the guts
into an empty wakefulness.
Roosting in the breadfruit trees,
the vultures scent adrenaline,
stretch the blackout of their wings.

Down by Ipanema, the beach
printed with light, curved as a thigh,
Will dances with a transvestite
from Argentina. She sings
Piaf, Marlene and the Stones,
eyes enamelled chrome-blue, too full
of keeping up appearances.

Rain for three days and without sleep,
we drink sugar-cane alcohol
with Mike from Bradford and his girl.
She plays cat's-cradle on his knees, her smile
fixed as the Queen's on watered paper.
'Look at her, see those paps,
young man. Fit as a butcher's dog. Ha!'
Through NHS black spectacles
he winks. Behind his back, the ocean
glitters, thin as caviar.

Women or men? Body-paint runs
blue vines over naked skin.
At the Grand Ball, the beautiful
arrive with godmothers, who watch
not for watchers, the poor voyeurs,
but for the nod, the finger's snap,
the crack of Washington's head on a bill.
In the wings they fix
the price of nights on calculators.

From the upper balconies,
the tourist guides and foreigners
applaud the lambada dancers,
and young bloods bow to the boxes
where old families and new men
observe from the leathered dark.
The band plays music without scores

in the pits, and the view from the gods
inked with the sepia of cigars.

Outside, we find a telephone,
call England. Happy something,
someone. Then wine from the Amazon
in rooms with golden wallpaper.
The liquor cures cancer, and burns—

Drums along Copacabana,
dealers and whores working the shades.
Where the sea ends, city begins—

Rio. The mango-man skins fruit
with a machete. Tells us God
took five days to finish this place,
one for the rest. Oil wells up from the soft flesh

and where the shanty-towns have slipped
from the hills in the slough of rain
a body in a ditch of trash
is not a tragedy for most:
death has no more drama
than poverty. Nothing worth waiting for.

Next morning we write postcards home
from the Sugar Loaf mountain
where hummingbirds turn the sun green.

Jael

They came away from our mountain wars
slow with the effort of losing a country.
Foreign men, armour-hulked. Trudging, blood
on their pelts. Outsiders, and that blood
of a different making.

Animals. Kneeling to drink, dog-lipped.
Only one cupped his hands and stood. Proud
as the axis lords of Philistine. A leader,
used to strength. Though horses, men and everything
broken in the war's clumsy rout.
Half-dead with knock and shield-butt.

Foreign as locusts. Still, I called him
Majesty. Sheltered him, burned my lamps
after dark, the shouts of troops
far as Jerusalem,
while the clouds skittled rain
over the scree of Ephraim.

He slept here on my bed. I think he dreamed
of his country. Temples carved
with Baals, green-tongued. His god the demon
of noontide and scorching summers.

After, when Israel had won
its valleys and the high passes
for the goats, the orators made words of me.
They praised the power in my forehead
and my workers' hands, although
it wasn't hard to do. The tent-peg sharp,
new pine, tanned with sap.
The tenting mallet solid yew.

The foreigner sunk in his sleep,
mosquitoes settling like knives
on his lips and where lank hair
thinned at the temples' cradle-bone.
To pick the stake and judge the blow—

No work, that. A single breath.
Lighter shift than pressing wine,
or camping on the desert plain.
The men gone, and the tents to pitch.

No work. I daydream of a king's skull.
My strength, his strength, his death.
And my hands itch.

Three Wishes in a Small Town

All day the hills smell of sawdust.
It makes him think of English girls
while he works the cork trees,
stripping them to the red wood:
white-shoes white-handbag-girls
waiting outside Cádiz hotels
with mouths that taste of cigarettes.
He knows their small-talk and their skins,
where they're smooth and where they're broken.

Now tonight his hands smell yellow with sawdust,
like the mouths of smokers.
He wipes them dry and drinks his thirst,
his thoughts, then his direction-sense,

watching the navigation-lights along the coast
of Africa. Listening to expatriates
talking down their homesickness;
the sheep as white as cricketers,
the cast-iron of clouds, and it's
long past midnight, while streetcats ooze like tar
between the fountain and the statue to the Civil War.

He drinks with them until they're gone,
then walks alone to the low-tide mark.
His feet on sand print watered light
between the wormcasts and seagulls.

He likes it here, where nothing talks.
He dreams of catching monkfish by their seabed gills
and when he wakes, his vomit tastes of salt and pearls.

The waves are seamed with light. He feels
clean. Cleaned-out
like gutted fish. The sand is warm. He'd give it all to eat
a plate of eggs. Their yolks and whites and shells.

The Mule and the Rain

I've been watching it all day
while the ice chimes odd times in my gin.
Waiting for something to happen.
In the field by the white hut

the mule is standing on hot bone
hooves. The trees around the house
are heavy with green oranges
and the cold belled clink of the goats
finding roots under the branches.

Siesta. Empty hills the colour
of grape-must, animal shit,
car-yard rust. The mule is propped,
shadow down between its feet,
on sagegrass yellowed as the skin of a meateater.

An old man in a flat cap, barefoot,
strings up red peppers to dry
on the walls of the white hut.
The wind disturbs them. Nothing else
moves. The mule leans its head out
so that the bones hold their weight.

I don't know what I'm looking at.
A mongrel, punched-black horse standing
all day without moving to eat,
not drinking. It's like watching tides
turning out, the way exposure
cures it like leather. The sun
breaking sweat across its back.

Midnight. I wake half-drunk from dreams of drought
to the lowtide smell of wet concrete,
rain churning in the carob trees.
I stand outside, under the eaves,
listening to the sigh of it,
and from the white hut, the sound of grieving,
on and on in the clarity of the night.

How to Light Dynamite

Mr Toumbi's second son, fire slopping from his hand,
throws an Easter cherry-bomb and runs. His flip-flops slap
   applause.
Crowds thicken in the streets. The air
is clear enough that bat-wings clap
loud as kid-gloves, shaken out.

The father pours out ouzo shots. Bottle-tin
clicks on glass. And all the time he's muttering.
I find it hard to make it out. He says his oldest granddaughter
was buried without hands. He asks
'You know how to light dynamite?'

Good Friday, and all afternoon
sea-foam cooks in the harbour-mouth.
Mrs Toumbi guts white squid, fries them into wedding-rings,
moves with drinks between old men
until they straighten and go home. Over the moorings,
rockets bloom. The sea is cooling like a stone.

'You know how to light dynamite?'
'No.' He wipes his face. Lights up.
His fingers smell of aniseed
and household poisons. The match smokes
like a thurible
in the half dark. 'Like this.'

Cigarette in his teeth,
fist clenched against the wince of ash.
Eyes clenched. 'Like this. To get the heat.
I never knew she smoked. They buried her
without hands.' Outside,

the sea shakes with a noise
like train-tracks. From the hills, the young town men
throw sparklers of dynamite.
The air is spiced with it. The town cistern
leans back and splits its sides.

The sky is turning sepia
with rock-dust. In the flashlit square
people dance and fall dancing,
debris on their clothes and faces.

Mrs Toumbi finds a glass,
sits with us. We drink until
the evening is almost silent
the merlins bat-hunting
over the navigation-point of Venus.

Flora and the Admiral

She keeps the knick-knacks clean like fruit
stacked fresh in a shop-front; shells sour
with brass and gunpowder,
apricot-sized barnacles,
sealed tins of cigarettes. At night,

drinking, not drunk, he sits
hard-backed in the hard-backed chair.
Circling the window's square,
he's pitched into the long head sea, rails
swept under greeny walls. His mouth is watertight.

Flora dusts, listening
to shipping forecasts. German Bight,
Maas Lightship, Scapa Flow. The Admiral
sees tall ships in emptied bottles.
He thinks of them like cathedrals,
lifeworks. The chiselled tongue of a saint
finished by the father's son.
Clinker-built to ironclad. Flora's standing,
back to the wall. He takes her in
like a pin-up unrolled in a mess-room.

She's watching how his body's aged
out of itself. Eyebrows hung clumped
like samphire, breath
in love with salt, skin oilskin, night-sweat
a synthesisation of tar

which she swabs at, smelling on him
the sweet tang of deck-iron
kettle-hot under heavy fire.

But breakfast's the time for remembering,

the kitchen window wide to hills
packed blue-green with cabbages, or
tideswells, frosted with rain

or his young hands, scrubbed of brine,
pulling her down into a pond of bluebells.

II

BACK TO THE CITY

London Pastoral

I want to tell you something:
for three nights now a bird has sung
in the road trees. A water song.
The neighbours are complaining; no one
knows what species the bird is. No one
even sees it. Pools coupons
titter against chain-links. Chip cartons
scuttle past time-delayed,
time-locked shopfronts. Then the bird
starts to sing.

You'll hear it with the window open,
even when the first rain gathers
to a downpour, hallways sweet
with the residue of road-tar.
Then you can grin, or watch me grin
at woodpigeons in wet weather
sat in the road trees, suffering
damp white collars. Like divorcees,
not looking at one another.

New Verses for Clock City Magpies

Eight for black, nine for white.
Ten for a step and its echo at night.
Eleven for credit, twelve for cash.
Thirteen for pickpockets milling the crush.

Fourteen for blackmail, fifteen for tax.
Sixteen for passion in cul-de-sacs.
Seventeen steps from the porch to the car.
Eighteen for life, with good behaviour.

Nineteen pounds ninety-nine pence-ful of lager.
Twenty plus tips for a blow and a popper.
Twenty-one faces pressed flat to the window.
Twenty-two magpies half-lost in shadow.

One for white, two for black.
Three chances left to guess why they attack.

North-West London, 8.15

It's closing time at the bloodmobile.
The oldest Camden derelict
still waits outside for chocolate,
her dirty-old-man coat and smile

lovely as a pub-crawl while she dreams of blood and
    peppermint.
She doesn't notice when the medic
locks the doors and drives away. She looks up from the
    pavement
at clouds the size of Regent's Park
and London's fourteen-hour sunset.

She's walking in her head between
Ten Bells, The Green Man and Blade Bone,
their smells and noise; extractor fans,
Special Tonite *chuck steak satay*,
the burn of Whiskey Flake Rubbed Ready,

velvet rooms stained blue with smoke
like fishtanks, where the couples grumble
together like grindstones
over the minutes of last trains
out into silences and evenings.

She gets as far as Venus No. 5
Off-Licence, Kentish Town. The steps are cold
but when she sits
still, over the taste of gin and rooftops
she can hear the chains
and see the cagework mountain outline

of Lord Snowdon's Aviary
where pelicans and sacred ibis
wink awake their ink-drop eyes
at every key that doesn't fit
each brakelight and every footstep
in the dead ends of Water Lane and Haven Street.

Love Song

Promise me something. Promise me
a kiss. Your lips are methedrine,
faster than alcohol. Swear on
the ram-raiders, the joyriders
garbaging up the night. Swear on
the Underground-surfers. Kiss me.

Come to me in the high places.
Kite Hill and the housing estates
where pensioners behind their lace
wait for your movements and your face.
Let them watch you come to me.

I love the roll of your sex
when you walk, and the black
of your belly after the talk.
Clearness of acts in the quick of the dark.

Show me your skin. Show me again.
Your clothes undone, your nakedness
and eyes open. Watching my face
for lust. Staring, their whiteness
makes my heart beat
you make my heart beat
by the whites of your eyes.

I touch your tears and have no words.
We crouch like borstal cases in stairwells
and cul-de-sacs. Your head back,
your throat open and no more
to give. Hands knotted in my hair. The stars
not burning down on us
like the songs of kings,
only burning. We make our own songs.

Broken Bone

Today the world is ugly:
through Holloway and Kentish Town
the bike bag-lady is riding
with a fishtank on her knees.
In the fishtank is a bone.
She stops outside the library.
She talks the snarl of wind in kitestring.

The world is ugly. The sky
looks like it cut the liver out
and burnt it. Days are when I get
like this. I need a friend all right, but
real friendship is rare. You must know that.

Today is Moss Side, yesterday
was North of Sunset. When I walk
I'm thinking of the girls who look
like something on a chocolate box.
Very chocolate. Chocolate milk.
I'm thinking of spring chicken skin,
peeling off like satin gloves.
Broken bone grinds its teeth
with my footsteps, quick slow quick.

Stop. The third house on the left
has caught my drift again. Sit down.
She's left the upstairs window open.
The fleshy chambers of my heart
wince ash like a cigarette.

The worst thing is how much I love the pain.

Playground at 2 am

What else are net curtains for?
Look. At least switch off the lights.
Call me a poet, call me a voyeur.
Behind the backs of mortgaged flats

the bulbs inside the lamp-post lamps are dark
as onions, and the playground dark
as the places between cities. Inch
the curtains open. There's the bench,

the swings, the wince of cigarettes,
their singe. Close your eyes, let them adjust.
Children are playing on the roundabouts.
You see? Fast hands, his denims down, her breast.

It's not exactly sexual, watching;
It's not exactly not.
Maybe it's a sex assault,
maybe it's remembrance,
to watch her face, his eyes. To try
and catch their features in my fingers.
Press your face against the glass;

they won't notice. Don't be shy,
everyone gets like this sometimes.
It's a kind of fear, it's something
to do with being us,

stopped in mid-step, unwatched, watching
where the action is.

Sheep's Clothing

'May God protect the lamb from the wolf' – (Spanish traditional hymn)

Don't get me wrong. Your face is smooth and soft
as clingfilm. But, my love, your voice has claws

and though (quite naturally) I'm pleased to say
that your fine hands do not resemble paws

there is a sweet, dark perfume on your breath
and I find I believe that it has teeth

—In many ways you look like death
warmed up. What is it that you keep

wound up, behind the puzzle-depth
of eyes that are so smiling bright?

I think there's wolf in your sheep's clothing,
but you wear the clothing well.

Come out with me. The city smells
of terrace cakes in terrace houses,
rented rooms and private halls,

the mathematics of small lives; a point
is that which can't be split,
a lifeline is length without breadth—

Will you come out with me? Tonight
the Underground shakes the pavement
and the moon is a heart's-width.

Xenophobia

Lock the door. Is it locked?
When he's trying to get in,
he waits outside the door, the black man,
close as shadow to a foot.

Come in, if you're going to.
Not from round here, are you?
Don't know it. Different street.
Did you get my order? Meat
goes underneath the fly-net. Milk?
Make us up a drink.

Mary. Without blood.
And my binoculars—
Don't think that I can't see, because
I can. Bring them here, if you could.

Do me a favour, jink the curtain back
a bit, to get the park
in. That's where the girls are.
Look at the way they walk, outsiders,
balancing themselves all day
against the whole sky—

I like binoculars, it's good
to focus in slowly. It means
you know where you are by the distance.
But don't look up, or you'll go blind.

Sometimes, when the chair is set
too close to the window, sunlight
warms my feet. I don't like how it
slides between my toes like egg-yolk.
I sit well back. Wait for dark.

I go out when I have to. Out.
Limbs trail from my brain like roots
uprooted from their element.
There's lots to see here. Silhouettes

precise in a dark room, casements
cross-referencing distant walls.
And there are always people out there,
old children. Daffodils
white as searchlights in the gloom.
Children circling to get home. That's their problem,

not mine. I'm home. I've measured it. I'm sure.
There's the spindled chain of the wind-chime,
its bell-shadow touching the foot of the door.

The Woman who Talks to Ezra Pound in Tesco

The woman who talks to Ezra Pound in Tesco
wants to know which bleach works best
to kill off mice in pipes. Pound doesn't know,
and the cashiers look past

her bulk and noise. She's taken down
five kinds of bleach, and now she can't
put them back up, because the dog
—curled prawn-like in her shopping-bag—won't wait,
and gets attacked alone.

Outside, semi-automatic cars
misfire in the suntraps of streets.
I help her with bottles. Today
she tells me to fuck off, they're hers.
Less often, recently, she waits
for recognition, then hugs me, calls me
lovely wee thing, so that I walk home
smelling of old piss, but thankful.

Today she tells me to fuck off.
I carry the dog anyway. It lolls its tongue
through the plastic bag handle.
She holds my arm for safekeeping.

'Have you read my poems? Listen. "Christ,
and when I sleep/ Your wounds hop on to me
Like little mice . . ." Do you know Mr Pound?'

I tell her no. An ice-cream van unwinds
between the tenements. Net curtains
dislodge screes of dust. A Bluebird, wheelblocked,
creaks in the heat and basks in rust.

Life Savings

The dead worry me.
My hands shake until I scrawl them
into balls of wastepaper
stuffed in the bottoms of pockets.
I'm older than my father.
I keep cash and receipts in separate wallets.

Four cans of Guinness, one of
Ambrosia creamed rice. Potatoes.
One lottery card. Nineteen,
thirteen, seven, three, three,
one.

Not all the best things here are free.
The girl who wraps my spuds in Sun
is London Indian Ugandan.
Teeth like radishes.
She marks up vegetables and fruit,
Asps, Obes, Qus. I could
stand to watch all day. I could.
But the day's getting on.

I don't mind paying. I don't hate
waiting to foot the bill, just
this mountain bike wheel, U-locked
next to the bus-stop all winter.
Spokes clipped, gears crowed out.
Nothing left except the tyre.
Unpunctured, still locked.

Here's the eyehole of my door,
here's the one easy chair.
I know what happens here and what

the cost will be. The carriage-clock, seeding
inside its greenhouse,

the grain-click of seconds.
I don't miss one. I can't listen. I keep the TV on.

After tea I crack a can,
wait for the morning programme.

Today the House is Full of Dishcloths

Today the house is full of dishcloths.
They pad staircases and loom blue
across back doors, hung out to dry.
The yard cats have got hold of one.
They worry it and leave it scrawled
on the steps like a half-dead bird.

Someone's crying in the hall,
coal-sack eyes pressed against
dishcloths. The kitchen drawers are packed
with four tin-openers, and dishcloths
scorch-marked, soft, screen-printed
with Rutland hedgerow birds no one
has ever heard. 'Old Father Thames Hotels'
where none of us has stayed.

At TV dinnertime, no one
asks for a serviette. We eat
tin-tray foods, emptying out
the new old freezer in the hall,
with ample dishcloths on our knees.
The house smells of asparagus
and there are small disturbances:

bookshelves cluttered with crocus-bulbs,
allotment onions, 'Pearl' light-bulbs.
Wooden coat-hangers are clumped
on door-knobs. Hung from one, there is
a black waistcoat we all try on,
but which will fit no one. The stairs
are cramped with family snapshots
catalogued in tight script,
a doctor's time-of-death handwriting—

portraits framed from distances.
It's hard to recognise faces.
Harder to search it all, and find
this one fine human frailty. Here:
blurred by proximity,

my grandfather's finger,
exposed in the foreground.

Reasons Why

Watch this—
Nothing in this hand, nothing
in this hand. In both hands,
something from nothing:

a poem, a wobble of bubble
pulled from the hoop
of a mouth or
from air-pressure

! Here. Eyes wide, look: blossom is
yoghurt-dollops, how it drips
petal-drops. Woodpecker is
a wooden ruler, plucked against
a wooden desk. This is a promise,

given and not kept—a riddle,
slapstick, scratch-and-sniff: bluebells
are fusepaper, gunpowdering
shadows of trees that snarl with traps
of kite-string. Words and silences
will fit to anything and lock
like indexes and thumbs in prayer
or stripes and grass-skin on a liger.

Tigering the pages, lines
printed deep as X-ray burns
or light as ripples in vanilla—

Why? Don't ask me why. Or ask why Les,
the next-door taxi-driver,
stole his wife a goldfish-bowl—
sized gaslight off Buckingham Palace.

Meat

She has another fall at Christmas.
It's while she's ironing,
and she remembers it because
the ironing-board falls on the phone.
Cracks the mouthpiece. Inside
she finds a wasp in the nest of wiring.
Yellow as a high-voltage warning.
Pressed in through the holes
to sleep. Sleepy. She holds it in her hand,
closes the hand into a fist.
It helps her concentrate.

She buys offcuts
and cuts them small,
breakfast, dinner and tea. That way
she gets to watch the box and eat
without missing the London sports.
But cutting's getting difficult.
She uses kitchen scissors first,
to snicker through the raw meat.

Small things go wrong
when they can. It's not senility,
the taps left choking
hot phlegm in dark rooms. The washing
piling up like nasty thoughts.
It all gets lost if she lets it. Pills especially.
It's just that she's got other things
to think about. One other thing.

King's Cross. Mice wince
between the tracks. She leans against
a tube-map. Listens for four-letter words. Watches
a pregnant woman sitting down,
smiling as the load eases. Bitch,
the bitch. She holds in her pain
like mouthfuls of paraffin.

Locks her teeth. If she gives in
it'll escape as laughter, then
ignite the city. No one moves.
Headphones hiss. Her knuckles crack.
There is a watchtick in her head,
a fuse inching towards its dynamite.

July 14th, 10 pm

The moon round as an oven-dial.
Ten fire-engines slide their red trombones
up past the Cock and Bottle
and the brink-lights of petrol-stations.

Behind windshields, linked by fax,
Neighbourhood Watch is watching me at work.
I'm looking for the depth of ink
to plus or minus hands or feet. I've found it in the index
of the Central Urban Zone Phonebook:

Jewson. Butler, Brick Lane. Skinner.
Butcher, E17. Blackborn. Blackburn. Black
stock, Market Place St. White City Under
takers, Inc. Rooks clot the branching hemispheres

of plane trees, and the London sky
confused with stagelight and small allergens.
I've lost the point again
of Indus mud in indigo, and the fear of lights-out

in blacklistings. On my side of the window,
a tentacle's shank and a goat's eye
retreat over sandbars and pages.
Or advance. It's hard to tell.
I can't hear a thing in the sirens' shadow.

The Beekeepers

Mr Salter walks across the garden like an astronaut;
washing-up gloves, white net suit.
Something has got inside the gloves.
He puts the slats of honey down, peels
pink rubber to the sting, the bee
looking for weaknesses.
He kills it when it gets upset.

The kitchen floor linoleum
is varnished with old wax. Our shoes
click like fingers. Mrs Salter
closes doors and net curtains.
Insects tumble at the windows,
bees the colour of honey,
wood the colour of honey
the air set yellow with the smell of it.

Outside, helicopters drone
over London. Mr Salter
peels wax from the comb
neat as appleskin. The slough
dropped away to show the bright
shine of something stolen, something

sweet and implicit with gain.
Mrs Salter makes tea,
butters cake, licks her thumb
clean of bittersweetness. Calm
holds us in its amber deadweight.
Mrs Salter pours for us;
she's mother here. My stomach growls. On her lap,
honey drips into the jar,
collecting dark. Transparency,
translucent now. Opaque.

Midnight in the City of Clocks

April, and this year April is
election month. In Rust Belt rooms
we wait for conditions and terms, the dark lit
television-blue. Wind rhymes along the thin tongues
of aerials and nothing moves outside except

downpour. But it's getting late.
I head down through the empty lots
of outbuildings, asphalt road wet
as hair plastered to a forehead.
In the Underground I find
tomorrow's newspapers and sit,
reading candidate predictions and the list
of polling stations. When there's nothing left to read
I try to sleep to kill the time
until midnight, when all the clocks
groan in their mainsprings with the need
for Summertime and difference.

I wake up to a car alarm. The station
coughs with subsidence.
The pavements hiss like fusepaper

and pouring from the ghettos, rain
acid as slag, and with it men
who live out of suitcases, men
who sleep with nylon suits pressed flat
under one-night mattresses.
All around the church clocktowers
the air shudders with hours.

0044 ·
208
452
4133

43 Midland Terrace
London
NW2 6QH
England